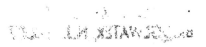

WHAT ARE NATURAL DISASTERS?

LOUISE SPILSBURY

Britannica®
Educational Publishing

IN ASSOCIATION WITH

ROSEN
EDUCATIONAL SERVICES

Published in 2014 by Britannica Educational Publishing (a trademark of Encyclopædia Britannica, Inc.) in association with The Rosen Publishing Group, Inc.
29 East 21st Street, New York, NY 10010

Distributed exclusively by Rosen Publishing.
To see additional Britannica Educational Publishing titles, go to rosenpublishing.com

First Edition

Britannica Educational Publishing
J.E. Luebering: Director, Core Reference Group
Anthony L. Green: Editor, Compton's by Britannica

Rosen Publishing
Hope Lourie Killcoyne: Executive Editor
Nelson Sá: Art Director

Library of Congress Cataloging-in-Publication Data

Spilsbury, Louise.
What are natural disasters?/Louise Spilsbury.
    pages cm. — (Let's find out: earth science)
Includes bibliographical references and index.
ISBN 978-1-62275-271-3 (library binding) — ISBN 978-1-62275-274-4 (pbk.) — ISBN 978-1-62275-275-1 (6-pack)
1. Natural disasters — Juvenile literature. I. Title.
GB5019.S68 2014
363.34 — dc23

    2013023019

Manufactured in the United States of America

CONTENTS

WILD EARTH

Most of the time and in most places in the world, Earth is quite safe. Now and then, however, Earth turns wild! A volcano erupts. An earthquake splits open the land. A flood covers fields and villages in raging water. Hurricanes blow down trees and homes.

Natural disasters are destructive events caused by forces of nature and not by people.

Floods destroy houses, making people homeless.

Natural disasters affect thousands of people every year. They cause injury and death. They destroy homes and buildings. We should never underestimate the power of nature.

THINK ABOUT IT
Look for patterns in the natural disasters you read about in this book. People have found ways to limit the damage such disasters cause.
Why then do natural disasters continue to happen, year after year?

VOLCANOES

A volcanic eruption happens when fountains of hot, melted rock, called lava, spurt out of a hole in Earth's surface.

When big volcanoes explode, they shoot out broken rocks along with lava. The rocks fall to the land, and smoke makes the air black.

Before lava escapes from the volcano it is known as magma.

The cone shape of a volcano is made up of layers of old lava from earlier eruptions.

The surface of Earth is a thin layer of hard rock called the crust. Below it is hot liquid rock called magma. A volcanic eruption begins when magma rises up through the crust. As it rises, the hot rock melts anything in its way, making a tunnel to the surface. Then the volcano erupts! Volcanic eruptions can be very destructive. But they can also create new landforms.

THINK ABOUT IT

What do you think the effect is when volcanoes cause eruptions under the sea? How do you think volcanic islands are created?

EARTHQUAKES

Earthquakes cause more damage than any other type of natural disaster. Small earthquakes make the ground tremble. They might shake a cup off a table. Large earthquakes can bring down buildings, crack open the ground, and buckle bridges. In a big earthquake, the land can ripple up and down like a wave on the sea.

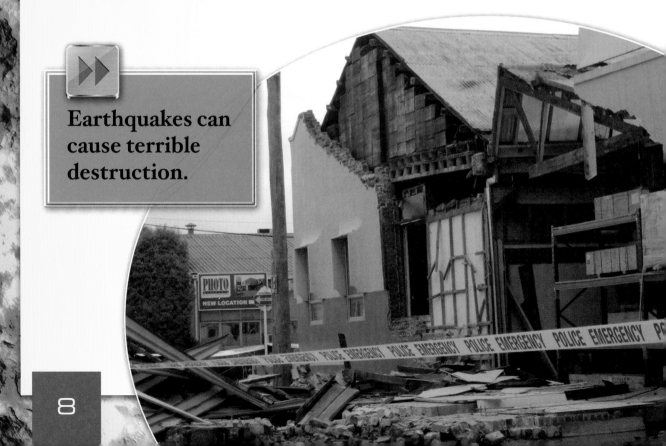

Earthquakes can cause terrible destruction.

Most earthquakes are caused by changes in Earth's outermost shell, or crust. The crust is made up of about a dozen rock masses called plates that are constantly moving. In different places they move apart, collide, or slide past each other. Over time, this movement causes great pressure to build up. When the pressure becomes too great, the rock masses shift along a crack in the crust, called a fault.

Earthquakes can open cracks, or faults, in Earth's crust.

COMPARE AND CONTRAST

What happens in a volcano? What happens in an earthquake? How are they alike? How are they different?

Tsunamis

A tsunami is a huge wave that becomes bigger as it comes closer to land. Tsunamis can be 100 feet (30 m) tall. They crash onto harbors and coasts as enormous walls of water. Tsunamis can wash boats onto land, and sweep away cars, buildings, and trees. They can bury fields and towns under water.

⏩ "Tsunami" comes from the Japanese words *tsu,* meaning harbor, and *nami,* which means wave.

Tsunamis can destroy almost anything in their path.

Tsunamis usually happen because of an earthquake on the ocean floor. If one of Earth's plates suddenly slips below the ocean floor, this sends an enormous shudder through the seawater. The shudder creates massive waves. Underwater volcanoes can also cause tsunamis. They happen when volcanic eruptions cause large blocks of ice or rock to fall and crash into the sea.

THINK ABOUT IT
How is the way that volcanoes and earthquakes cause tsunamis similar?

11

Hurricanes

Hurricanes are forceful, destructive storms. They begin over warm seas. The warm water heats up the air just above it. When air heats up, it becomes lighter and rises. Cooler air fills the space the warm air leaves behind. This creates winds. When hot air rises quickly, the winds move faster and start to spin. When the winds spin quickly, they become a hurricane.

Hurricanes, also known as typhoons and cyclones, are a kind of tropical cyclone. A tropical cyclone is a circular storm that forms over a warm ocean.

In the United States in 2012, Hurricane Sandy damaged gas lines and started fires that destroyed houses.

Some hurricanes stay over the ocean. They can whip up massive waves that cause floods. Others move at high speed toward land. The strong winds and the heavy rain hurricanes bring can last for days or weeks. Hurricanes can blow down buildings, move automobiles, and uproot trees.

To **uproot** something is to pull it out of the ground.

TORNADOES

A tornado is a spinning tower of air that twists down to the ground from a thunderstorm cloud. Most tornadoes are small, last for a few seconds, and do no damage. A few are hundreds of feet wide and miles tall, and can last for several hours. Like huge vacuum cleaners, they suck up everything in their way, and drop it down again later.

▶▶ The visible column of a tornado is called a funnel cloud.

Tornadoes start above land during a storm when warm, wet winds from one direction meet colder, drier winds coming from another direction. The warm air rises over the cold air and starts to spin. The rising, spinning air sucks in warm air from just above the ground. This warm air rises and makes the tornado higher and higher. The winds of a tornado are the strongest on Earth.

In 2013, a tornado devastated the city of Moore, Oklahoma.

COMPARE AND CONTRAST

How are tornadoes and hurricanes similar? How are they different?

Floods

When water overflows onto dry land, a flood takes place. Floods can happen without any warning. Large amounts of water are very heavy, and when water moves fast, it can be extremely forceful. When water suddenly floods an area of land, it can wash away people, cars, and other objects. Floods also fill buildings with water and mud, and cover fields, destroying the crops that grow there.

A flood can move very quickly, so people cannot drive away from it. It is best to move to high ground to escape.

Many people think of a **monsoon** as a drenching summer rain. However, a monsoon is actually the wind pattern that causes such rains.

Some floods happen when a lot of rain falls in a short time. The rain fills rivers until they spill over their banks. In Asia and Africa, heavy rain falls during the monsoon season, causing floods. Some floods happen when tsunamis or large waves caused by hurricanes hit land.

17

AVALANCHES

An avalanche is a large amount of snow that moves quickly down the side of a mountain. The avalanche can knock down everything in its path.

When an avalanche hits trees, rocks, and other objects with great force, it often drags them along. When it reaches the bottom of a mountain, the avalanche can bury whole towns in thick, heavy snow.

An avalanche can race down a slope as fast as a racing car!

Some avalanches happen after it has rained. When an area of snow gets very wet and heavy, it can suddenly slide down a slope. Avalanches can also happen when there are heavy winds or after it has been snowing heavily. People trapped under avalanches can die of hypothermia if they are not rescued quickly.

Avalanche rescue teams have dogs and special equipment to find people buried under the deep snow.

Hypothermia is when a person's body gets so cold it starts to shut down.

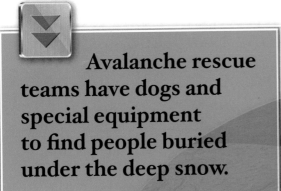

Landslides

A landslide is when large amounts or rock, soil, or mud slip suddenly down a hill or slope. Some landslides move slowly, but others can race downhill very quickly. When large amounts of rock and mud roll down a slope, they knock things down. Whole towns at the bottom of slopes can be buried in mud during a landslide.

Landslides can bury houses in wet mud, which then dries and sets hard, like concrete.

COMPARE AND CONTRAST

How are landslides and avalanches similar? How are they different?

When landslides cover roads, it makes it difficult for rescuers to reach victims.

Landslides happen when a layer of earth or rocks separates from the layer below it. Gravity pulls the loose layer downward. Mud on a slope can collapse when heavy rains make it soft and heavy. People can cause landslides when they cut down trees on a slope. Tree roots help fix the soil to a slope. Without them, soil slides easily downhill.

Wildfires

A wildfire is an uncontrolled fire that spreads through a wide area of forest, bushes, or grasses.

Some wildfires start when lightning strikes dry plants. However, people start most wildfires, usually accidentally. They can start when campfires get out of control or are not put out properly when people leave. Some fires start when people drop burning cigarettes.

Lightning is a flash of electricity produced by a thunderstorm.

Once a wildfire starts, it can spread quickly through a dry forest.

THINK ABOUT IT

Why do you think there are more wildfires after a long spell of very hot, dry weather?

Firefighters work hard to put out wildfires before they get close to people's homes.

After a wildfire starts, the flames spread quickly from plant to plant. A wildfire soon gets out of control. Large wildfires last for several days and destroy many plants. They also kill the animals that live among the plants. Wildfires that reach towns can kill people, too.

DROUGHTS

A drought is when a place gets little or no rain for a long period of time. Droughts happen most often in places that are already hot and dry, such as parts of the United States, Australia, and Africa.

Without water, soil becomes dry and begins to crack. Plants need water to live, so they start to die when soil dries out.

Plants cannot remain alive in very dry ground.

Drought has killed more people than any other type of natural disaster. If a drought happens in a poor country, people cannot buy water from elsewhere. When plants die, there is no food for farm animals or people to eat. Without plants such as corn and animals such as cows to eat, people go hungry and may die.

THINK ABOUT IT

All living things need water to survive. What do plants and animals use water for?

In a drought, it is difficult to give animals the water they need to live.

Blizzards

A blizzard is a powerful snowstorm that brings strong winds and lots of snow and ice. In a blizzard, winds blow at 35 miles per hour (56 km/h) or faster for at least three hours. Winds swirl ice and snow around in the air, causing low visibility. This makes it difficult for people to see where they are going.

▶▶ Blizzards cause lots of traffic accidents.

Low visibility is when you cannot see very far ahead of you.

People use bulldozers to clear snowdrifts from streets.

Blizzard winds blow snow into huge piles called snowdrifts. If heavy snowdrifts build up on houses, they can cause roofs to collapse. Snowdrifts also block roads and trap people in their homes, so they cannot travel to get food. Snowdrifts can be so deep that they can bury houses and trains. If someone is trapped outdoors, they might die of hypothermia.

Be Prepared

There may be more natural disasters in the future because of **climate change**. As Earth gets hotter, there will be more fires and droughts. When ice at the Poles melts, the level of the sea will rise and cause floods. We can reduce the risk of climate change by using fewer fossil fuels.

Climate change is the increase in Earth's temperature caused partly by people burning fuels such as coal and oil.

Venice, Italy, and other coastal places will flood more often if sea levels rise.

These defenses help to protect the coast of Florida from giant waves caused by hurricanes.

People can take steps to reduce the risk of natural disasters. People in areas where tornados are common build safe shelters in which to hide until a tornado has passed by. People build special fences on mountain slopes to stop avalanches. Everyone can learn what to do to keep safe if a natural disaster strikes in their area.

Glossary

crops Plants grown for food.

crust The layer of hard rock that forms the surface of Earth.

defenses Barriers made from rocks or sand to protect something, such as a beach.

erupts When a volcano explodes and hot, melted rock, called lava, spurts out of it.

flood When normally dry areas of land are suddenly covered in water.

fossil fuels Coal, oil, and natural gas formed millions of years ago from the remains of dead plants and animals.

gravity A pulling force that works across space.

lava Fiery hot, melted rock from inside Earth.

magma Molten rock material within Earth.

natural disasters Terrible events, such as tornadoes, hurricanes, or floods, caused by forces of nature, not people.

plates Giant pieces of rock that float on the hot, melted rock in the center of Earth.

Poles The ends of Earth. There is a North Pole and a South Pole.

roots The parts of a plant that anchor it into the ground.

season The time of year that has a particular weather pattern, such as summer or winter.

shelters Safe places, for example, underground, where people can go during a tornado.

snowdrifts Huge banks or piles of snow.

thunderstorm A storm with loud bangs of thunder and flashes of lightning as well as heavy rain.

weather The conditions of the air around us. For example, the weather can be hot or cold, dry or wet, sunny or cloudy.

FOR MORE INFORMATION

Books

Burgan, Michael. *Surviving Earthquakes* (Children's True Stories: Natural Disasters). North Mankato, MN: Raintree, 2011.

Fecher, Sarah and Clare Oliver. *Freaky Facts About Natural Disasters.* Lanham, MD: Cooper Square Publishing, 2006.

Parker, Steve and David West. *Natural Disasters: Moving Earth* (The Science of Catastrophe). New York, NY: Crabtree Publishing Company, 2011.

Walker, Sally M. *Volcanoes* (Early Bird Earth Science). Minneapolis, MN: Lerner Publishing Group, 2007.

Watts, Claire and Trevor Day. *Natural Disasters* (DK Eyewitness Books). New York, NY: DK Publishing, 2012.

Websites

Due to the changing nature of Internet links, Rosen Publishing has developed an online list of Websites related to the subject of this book. This site is updated regularly. Please use this link to access the list:

http://www.rosenlinks.com/lfo/natd

 INDEX